T0161420

THE
MINDFULNESS
COACH

Also in the Pocket Coach series:

THE CALM COACH

◆

THE CONFIDENCE COACH

◆

THE KINDNESS COACH

◆

THE POSITIVITY COACH

◆

THE SLEEP COACH

A Pocket Coach

THE MINDFULNESS COACH

GILL THACKRAY

Michael O'Mara Books Limited

This book is dedicated to Viv Dutton, my twin sister, for a lifetime's supply of encouragement, support, positivity and coffee.

First published in Great Britain in 2020 by
Michael O'Mara Books Limited
9 Lion Yard
Tremadoc Road
London SW4 7NQ

A CIP catalogue record for this book is available from the British Library.

Papers used by Michael O'Mara Books Limited are natural, recyclable products made from wood grown in sustainable forests. The manufacturing processes conform to the environmental regulations of the country of origin.

ISBN: 978-1-78929-252-7 in hardback print format
ISBN: 978-1-78929-254-1 in ebook format

1 2 3 4 5 6 7 8 9 10

www.mombooks.com
Follow us on Twitter @OMaraBooks

Cover and design by Ana Bjezancevic
Typeset by Claire Cater

Printed and bound in China

MIX
Paper from
responsible sources
FSC® C016973

CONTENTS

▼▼▼

INTRODUCTION

Mindfulness has surged in popularity over the past decade. Jon Kabat-Zinn, professor emeritus and founder of the Stress Reduction Clinic at the Center for Mindfulness at the University of Massachusetts Medical School, has done much to bring mindfulness to a wider audience.

Kabat-Zinn developed a mindfulness programme while working with patients experiencing conditions as diverse as chronic pain, anxiety, depression, heart disease, psoriasis and sleep problems. His clinical work had impressive results, producing improvements in both physical and psychological symptoms. His work eventually led to what we know today as the Mindfulness-Based Stress Reduction (MBSR) programme, bringing mindfulness into the mainstream.

Modern life has evolved in such a way that we are constantly connected. We have hundreds of different ways to engage with the world at unprecedented speed. We're pushed into multitasking – doing more than one thing at a time, while thinking about the next thing on our list. We eat while watching TV. Drive and listen to the radio. Walk and listen to a podcast. There's little time to stop and notice much along the way. It's easy to get caught up in our thoughts, becoming alienated from ourselves and those around us.

Living on autopilot leaves us barely aware of the nuanced mental, emotional and physical processes taking place within us. It's a disconnection that has taken place almost by stealth. Life on cruise control diminishes the natural joy that we experience when we're able to live in the moment.

Mindfulness gives us a choice. It provides us with a way of knowing what is happening as it's happening, reducing the volume of external noise. It is being fully aware and present in a world that constantly pulls at your attention with a multitude of distractions. When you're mindful, you're focusing your attention on purpose and without judgement. When we become more aware of the present moment, our thoughts and emotions, we are better able to understand ourselves. Pressing pause enables you to begin to see thoughts for what they are: mental events, rather than facts set in stone. This enables you to loosen the control of unhelpful habitual thinking.

When we're mindful, we use areas of our brain that are inactive on autopilot. Studies have found that mindfulness changes the physical structure of your brain. The brains of regular meditators look very different to non-meditators. Long-term meditators have literally transformed their brains. The mindful brain looks and behaves differently. Regular mindfulness practice results in an enormous range of physical and mental health benefits.

▲▲▲

A WAY OF

recentering

OURSELVES

◆ WHAT IS MINDFULNESS? ◆

Paying attention

Mindfulness is awareness of what is happening as it is happening. When you're mindful, you're not ruminating on the past or thinking about the future or the things you have to do. Instead, you are bringing your full attention to each moment. Mindfulness is paying attention to your thoughts, the sensations in your body, your feelings and what is going on in the environment around you. Jon Kabat-Zinn's classic definition says: 'Mindfulness means paying attention in a particular way: on purpose, in the present moment, and non-judgmentally.'

Mindfulness myths

Sometimes myths and misinformation surround mindfulness. These can be off-putting if you want to try it. Let's dispel some of those myths here.

- Mindfulness is not about emptying your mind. It's about focusing on what is happening as it happens. Your brain creates thoughts – that's what it does (and that's okay).

- Being mindful will not prevent you from achieving your goals, diminish your 'grit' or render you passive.

- You don't have to sit on the floor cross-legged.

- Mindfulness isn't always relaxing. Sometimes you might feel relaxed, at other times it can be challenging.

- You don't need to be mindful all the time.

- Mindfulness isn't a religion.

- You don't need to be silent to practise mindfulness.

- Mindfulness is only useful for mental health? Not true. Mindfulness is used in many walks of life including health, work, sport and creativity.

From 'doing' to 'being'

We spend so much of our lives trapped in busyness. We're constantly engaged in a goal-oriented 'doing mode'. We need to get things done and that becomes our focus. Thinking about what we need to do next takes priority. This constant striving leaves us feeling exhausted by the impossible task of keeping up.

We become preoccupied with our mental 'to do' lists, or turning things from the past over and over in our minds even though they have already happened. Think of 'doing mode' as cruise control for your brain; we actually notice very little of what is really going on.

When you're in driven, *doing* mode, you're not *being*. You develop habitual thought patterns and mental shortcuts in your busy mind. Sometimes those thought patterns can be negative or ruminative. By cultivating mindfulness, you can begin to recognize those thought patterns and choose where you place your focus. This is known as 'being mode'.

When you're in 'being mode' you're fully in the present moment. In being mode, we're not striving or constantly evaluating what is happening. There is no goal to achieve. We allow life to unfold with acceptance as we connect to each moment.

Practice: one-minute 'doing' to 'being'

Make yourself comfortable and see if it's possible to be in the moment for one minute. There's nowhere to go. There's nothing to do, except allow each second to unfold. Notice what is going on for you. What do you hear? What can you see? Are you aware of any physical sensations? Do you notice aromas? See what's here, right now.

You might find that you get distracted, or your mind wanders. Perhaps you'll notice thoughts coming and going. That's what the mind does – and it's okay. There's nothing wrong. When you notice that you've been distracted, gently let go of the distraction. If it helps, notice the thought or distraction and label it 'thinking'.

▲ ▲ ▲

◆ THE ORIGINS OF MINDFULNESS ◆

Mindfulness isn't new. It has been practised for thousands of years in Eastern philosophy. The roots of mindfulness are in Hinduism and Buddhism and can be traced as far back as 535 BC. Today, mindfulness has been embraced by mainstream society. You don't need to be religious to be mindful.

There is much debate around whether it is possible to remove Buddhism from mindfulness and whether we should even attempt to. Some practitioners claim that mindfulness has been diluted and commodified, creating what Ron Purser, professor of management at San Francisco University, refers to as 'McMindfulness'. He argues that the practice is being used as a sticking plaster without addressing the root causes of modern-day stressors, especially in the workplace.

While we need to guard against using mindfulness to reinforce and passively accept all that might be wrong with the world, it's important to retain what might improve individual and collective wellbeing.

Mindfulness can help us to create a better life for ourselves and our communities. For this reason, mindfulness is now used as a secular practice in a variety of fields.

➤ WHO IS USING IT AND WHY? ◆

Public interest in mindfulness has escalated over the last two decades. Alongside the clinical applications of mindfulness that Jon Kabat-Zinn pioneered, mindfulness is now used in a wide number of contexts. You can find mindfulness programmes in schools, the workplace, healthcare settings, the military, sport, law enforcement and even politics.

◆ THE BENEFITS OF MINDFULNESS ◆

The benefits of practising mindfulness have been well documented and are empirically supported. Many studies have found that mindfulness reduces stress, anxiety and depression. Researchers know that mindfulness can be as effective as antidepressants for some people; in fact, it is the National Institute for Health and Care Excellence's (NICE) choice of treatment for people who have had more than three recurring bouts of depression. Some of the benefits of mindfulness include:

- Decreased depression

- Pain management

- Help with anxiety

- Reduced rumination

- Stress reduction

- Improved focus

- Better memory

- Increased cognitive flexibility

- Less emotional reactivity

- Increased wellbeing and happiness

- Relationship satisfaction

Mindfulness provides enormous benefits for many people; however, there are some caveats.

◆ REASONS NOT TO BE MINDFUL ◆

Despite the many benefits of mindfulness, it isn't a panacea. Some of the research claims that you may see in the press or online have very little solid evidence behind them. For people with particular mental health issues, there may be an increased likelihood of adverse effects from mindfulness. Good Practice Guidelines suggest that for some people with pre-existing mental health difficulties – for example, a tendency to anxiety or depression, or a history of trauma or psychosis – the risk of experiencing an adverse event may increase when practising mindfulness. More research in the field is needed to find out why.

The potential downside of mindfulness is often overlooked. The analogy of physical exercise can help us to understand why this might be. If you hadn't done any form of exercise for years, you wouldn't decide to run a marathon straight away, without any training. Sometimes when we do train, physical exercise presents risk. We pull tendons, sprain muscles or injure ourselves. That doesn't mean that exercise is dangerous, or bad for us. For the vast majority of us, exercise is extremely beneficial for our physical and mental health.

The same is true of mindfulness. Think of it as a workout for your brain. When we first begin to practise, we may start to focus on things that we don't normally examine. It's like shining a light on areas of your life that you might have left in the dark up until this point, deciding to ignore. That might stir up uncomfortable feelings for us. It is better to start small with basic mindfulness practices rather than diving straight into a twelve-day silent retreat.

Current studies indicate that practising mindfulness doesn't cause mental health problems, but it may exacerbate pre-existing conditions. If you have concerns, it's always important to take a look at your national mindfulness teaching guidelines and speak to a qualified teacher before you begin.

✦ MINDLESSNESS ✦

Mindlessness is the opposite of mindfulness. It is not being aware of what is happening around you. It's when your mind wanders or you zone out and is sometimes referred to as autopilot. To a certain extent, this is the way that human beings are 'wired'. If we had to think about everything that we do, life would be impossibly hard work. There are some basic physical functions such as breathing or walking that we do automatically. We usually don't need to think about these actions; they simply happen without much thought.

There's nothing wrong with you if you recognize that you're sometimes on autopilot – most of us are. It's when we habitually occupy this space that it can begin to reduce our enjoyment of life. Autopilot robs us of our time, leaving us feeling permanently switched on and drained. Mindfulness helps us to recognize that we've become trapped in mindlessness and offers us an alternative to this state.

THE DEFAULT MODE NETWORK (DMN)

Marcus Raichle, a neurologist at Washington University, discovered that, even when we think we're resting, our brains are constantly churning and whirring away. He called this state the 'default mode network'. So, you might be wondering, what's the problem with that?

Sometimes we get trapped in this state of mindlessness. Maybe you already recognize it? We switch onto the DMN without being aware that we're doing it. This is when you lose touch with what is happening around you. You're no longer in the driving seat. The feeling that you are constantly playing catch up is a major clue. Consider the following scenarios and how often you find yourself in them:

- You wake up and immediately begin thinking about all of the things that you need to do.

- After a regular commute, you can't remember the journey.

- You're talking to someone, nodding your head and realize that you have missed huge chunks of the conversation.

- You eat your lunch at your desk as you work. You don't really taste your food and barely register that you have eaten.

- You rush from one task to another, constantly running through your 'to do' list in your head.

- You try to multitask but never seem to finish anything.

- Time flies by and you wonder where it went.

If that sounds like a fairly typical day, you've experienced mindlessness. When we are in DMN it's easy to get stuck there. It's also exhausting. Being on autopilot means that we're no longer making conscious choices. We become habituated, doing things without thinking.

Being mindful means that we are able to identify when we're on autopilot and intentionally disengage from it. We become more conscious of where we place our focus and are able to make choices that serve us well. Autopilot presents us with fertile ground on which to practise mindfulness. Researchers have found that the brains of people who practise mindfulness regularly wander less. They are more readily able to recognize when they're in DMN, and instead choose where they place their attention.

· · · · · · · · · · · · · · · ● · ● · ● · · · · · · · · · ·

Mindful practice: disrupting autopilot

Now that you recognize autopilot and the mindlessness that leads to it, what can you do about it? Take a handful of everyday, routine activities and see if it's possible to move out of the DMN and into mindful present moment awareness.

1. **Constant connection. Decide when you want to use your phone and when you don't. One of the most common examples of getting caught**

up in mindlessness is the reluctance to be parted from our phone.

2. Get wet. When you shower or bathe, notice the warmth of the water, how it feels against your skin. If you're using shower gel or soap, inhale the aroma. Feel your body relaxing as the water glides over you.

3. Beginner's mind. Choose an object that you are familiar with. It could be a jacket, a pair of shoes, an item of furniture or a book. Imagine that you are seeing, touching and feeling that object for the very first time. This is a way of bringing awareness to things that you might ordinarily ignore.

- -

METACOGNITION: WHY YOUR THOUGHTS ARE JUST THOUGHTS

How we relate to the thoughts that emerge when we're on autopilot can influence our mood. The truth is that your thoughts are not 'you'. They are not facts (however much we might believe that they are). Thoughts are mental events that emerge in our mind. One of the things that mindfulness helps us to do is to recognize our thoughts as such, rather than an accurate representation of reality. They're automatic; they come and go uninvited.

Think of your thoughts as a TV screen running in the background on low volume. An internal narrative chattering through the day, masquerading as rational fact. 'What's wrong with you?' it might ask. 'This is going to be terrible,' it informs you. 'I'll never be able to...' We might then decide to think about those thoughts in more detail and wonder what's wrong with us, creating a downward spiral. That's how our thoughts suck us into believing that they're real, creating a cycle of negativity.

When we recognize that thoughts are simply thoughts, not facts, we are able to deal with them more skilfully. We can choose which thoughts we engage with (and which we don't). But how?

- Take a couple of breaths. Imagine you are sitting by the side of a stream watching the water flow by. As each thought comes, picture it as a leaf floating along on the water. You notice it emerge and observe as it flows by. Notice and accept the thoughts without judging them as 'good' or 'bad'. Then watch them float away down the stream. Observe each passing thought in this way.

- Acknowledge the thought and ask yourself: Where's the evidence? Is this thought 100% true? Is it accurate? Might there be another way of looking at it?

- Ask yourself: What would things look and feel like if I didn't believe this automatic thought?

MAKING ROOM FOR MINDFULNESS IN A BUSY LIFE

One of the myths about mindfulness is that you need to spend hours doing it. There are many ways that you can build mindful moments into your life. See 'Mindfulness for when you're too busy' (pages 99–106) for more.

▲▲▲

YOUR BRAIN

on

MINDFULNESS

◆ TRAINING YOUR BRAIN ◆

The scientific community used to assume that our brains stopped developing when we're still young, and that what you're born with, you're stuck with. We now know that's not true. Mindfulness is like a workout for your brain. In the same way that we keep our bodies healthy and well by exercising, we can do exactly the same for our grey matter by being more mindful.

WHAT IS HAPPENING IN ◆ YOUR BRAIN WHEN YOU ◆ PRACTISE MINDFULNESS?

Researchers have found that regular mindfulness practice has multiple benefits for your brain. The activity in the amygdala (the part of the brain responsible for your 'fight, flight or freeze' response) is dampened down when you practise mindfulness. That means that you're less likely to have badly thought-through, knee-jerk reactions when things go wrong. Instead, mindfulness has been linked to increases in activity in the parietal lobe and the prefrontal cortex (PFC). The parietal lobe and PFC work together. The parietal lobe acts as the hub for our somatic (bodily) senses. It carries out a variety of functions, including processing sensory information along with other cognitive tasks. The PFC sits at the front of the parietal lobe and is the region of the brain associated with controlling emotions, problem-solving, planning and clear thinking. It's the part that we need to use more if we want to make effective decisions.

NEUROPLASTICITY: ◆ HOW MINDFULNESS ◆ SHAPES YOUR BRAIN

Research over the last two decades has demonstrated that the brain is able to change, adapt and make new connections throughout our lives. This process is called neuroplasticity. Your brain is malleable: it can change, develop and be reshaped.

Professor Richard Davidson took a look inside the brain and discovered that it's possible to 'rewire' it. We now know our brains can change in response to new events and experiences. Neurons and neural networks in the brain are able to change and reorganize when we experience something new. What's more, Professor Davidson discovered that regular mindfulness practice is one of the most effective ways to harness neuroplasticity. This has benefits for your brain and your body.

MINDFULNESS AND THE MIND-BODY CONNECTION

For many years, scientists used to view the mind and body as separate entities. Professor Alan Jasanoff describes this as a false dichotomy. We now know that there is a powerful interrelationship between the mind and the body. Our emotions, thoughts and feelings can have a profound biological impact upon the health and wellness of our bodies. Cultivating mindfulness helps us to become more intentional with our thoughts, improving our overall wellbeing. Regular practice will also help you to identify physical sensations and embodied emotions.

✦ LISTENING TO YOUR BODY ✦

The physical sensations in your body are always sending you information. We just don't always hear them. Mindfulness is a way of reconnecting with your body, of being able to recognize when it's telling you something. Aching shoulders could be a sign of stress. That's information telling you to dial down your stress levels with a mindful walk or a mindfulness practice that soothes you.

When you eat mindfully you may begin to notice that some foods make you lethargic or lower your mood. When you learn to identify those messages you can use that information to make different choices. Skilfully listening to your body is a way of opening up those channels of communication between the brain and the body.

Listening to your body can sometimes be complex. If you have suffered trauma in the past, it's important to work with a qualified mindfulness teacher who has experience of working with physical and psychological injuries. A knowledgeable teacher will be able to guide you in safe mindful body practices.

MINDFULNESS AND STRESS MANAGEMENT

We've looked at how mindfulness reduces the activity in a part of your brain called the amygdala. This is the part of the brain that is responsible for your response to stress. When you regularly give your brain a mindful workout, you are building your ability to manage stressful situations more effectively.

Learning to become more aware of your thoughts is the first step to managing your stress response more skilfully. Studies have found that stress diminishes our body's white blood cell response to infection. This is one of the reasons that mindfulness is widely used as a way of reducing stress. Our brains are key to how we perceive and interact with the world around us. Managing stress is an important part of remaining well.

· · · · · · · · · · ● ● ● ● ● · · · · · · · · · · ·

Practice to curate
your stress response

Once you become more mindful, you'll begin to get better at noticing times when you're stressed or anxious. Think about how you can build more mindfulness into your day at regular intervals to check in and see how you're feeling. This will help you to become familiar with your emotions, to tune into them, learning the best way to manage them. Curate a set of mindfulness practices that you can draw upon when you need to reduce stress, self-soothe or be more compassionate towards yourself (or others). There are many ways that you can begin to do this.

▲ ▲ ▲

S.T.O.P.

Set an alert to remind you to check in every hour or so and do this S.T.O.P. practice. This will help you to develop mindful awareness. It can be brief and done in sixty seconds or less.

1. Stop: **Stop whatever you are doing in this moment. Stop 'doing' and bring your mind into 'being' mode. Notice the present moment, right now.**

2. Take a breath: **Breathe in and breathe out. Breathe naturally, bringing your attention to your breath. Notice the cycle of breath as you inhale and exhale.**

3. Observe: **Focus on your thoughts and emotions. Gently notice what's happening in your body. Stay curious about what you notice without judging it.**

4. Proceed: **What feels like an appropriate way to proceed? Move on mindfully.**

▲▲▲

GETTING
down to
MINDFULNESS

◆ MINDFULNESS PROGRAMMES ◆

There is an enormous variety of available mindfulness programmes. Either online or in person, these can provide invaluable support to anyone who wants to develop a regular practice. Another benefit of attending a course is that you'll have access to a teacher who can answer your questions and provide support. See 'Finding a teacher', page 116.

Two of the most widely known programmes are the Mindfulness-Based Stress Reduction (MBSR) course and the Mindfulness-Based Cognitive Therapy programme (MBCT). In addition to these there are many Mindfulness-Based Living (MBL) courses along with a plethora of related courses including creativity, cooking and so on.

▲▲▲

FORMAL AND INFORMAL PRACTICE

Mindfulness practice can very loosely be divided into formal and informal practice. Formal practice involves setting time aside where you focus entirely on meditation. You can do this sitting or lying down. Meditations that you might use for formal practice could include mindful breathing, a body scan (a mindfulness practice that involves bringing your focus to what is happening in your physical body) or mindful movement. This might not always be possible. Either you won't have time or you don't want to commit to a formal daily practice. That's when informal practice can be useful.

Informal practice consists of building mindfulness into your regular, daily activities. This is where you bring mindfulness to something that you ordinarily do without thinking about it. We'll examine informal practices throughout this book but, essentially, they are a relaxed awareness of the present moment. You've already used one when you practised 'beginner's mind' (see page 23).

Informal mindfulness could include drinking a cup of coffee, cooking, or really listening to someone that you are talking with.

Whether you engage in formal or informal mindfulness, it's important to start where you are. Sixty seconds is always better than nothing and you might find that, once you begin, it's surprisingly easy to increase the amount of time that you are able to commit to daily.

ESTABLISHING A REGULAR PRACTICE

Often, when you start to set time aside for mindfulness, you'll be advised to stick to the same time and place every day. While this is great advice in terms of habit formation, many of us just don't live that kind of life. Schedules change along with demands on your time. It may be much kinder and more realistic to be less rigid than that. If you can have a regular mindfulness slot in your day, great. If not, it's okay to be flexible.

HOW LONG SHOULD I MEDITATE FOR?

Like anything else when you first begin, it's important to take small steps. If you were beginning to take up physical exercise you wouldn't run a marathon on the first day. It's exactly the same when it comes to mindfulness. Start small and build on your practice from there. It's important that it feels doable. Anything that feels like a gargantuan chore is likely to send you into avoidance mode.

If five or ten minutes each day feels comfortable, begin there. Known as 'micro-dosing', these small doses of mindfulness will still provide benefits. You're more likely to stick at it and develop a regular practice as a result. The jury is out in terms of the science on exactly how long is best. What we do know is that regular practice every day is more beneficial than trying to cram a long session in every week. Do what feels comfortable for you.

▲ ▲ ▲

KNOWING WHERE YOU'RE GOING

Setting an intention before you meditate will help you to focus. An intention isn't a goal – remember that we're trying to step away from striving mode – it's more of a purpose. Aligning your values with your intention helps you to direct your attention with purpose. It's like using a map for your mindfulness practice.

Setting an intention

Time: three to five minutes

Find a comfortable position, either in a chair or on the floor. Follow your breath, as best you can. Begin to notice what happens as you breathe in and breathe out. Settle into a gentle breathing rhythm without trying to alter your natural breath. Once you have begun to focus on your breath, turn your focus towards setting an intention. What do you want to create in this moment? Think about why you want to be more mindful.

Your intention could be an area of your life that you would like to cultivate, for example:

◄ *My intention is to be more in the moment.* ►

◄ *I would like to be more compassionate.* ►

◄ *My intention is to feel less caught up in my thoughts.* ►

You might even choose to set an intention for each day as well as for your mindfulness practice.

Rest in your curiosity for a moment or two. Where are you able to align your values with your purpose for meditating right now? Perhaps you would like to be kinder to others (or yourself), less stressed, more resilient or more compassionate.

When your intention emerges, say it to yourself and begin your meditation.

Create your own intention

◄ *My intention is...* ►

◄ *Today I intend to...* ►

Some people choose not to set an intention, preferring instead to simply 'be' as they meditate. Do what works for you.

· · · · · · · · · · · · ● ● ● ● ● · · · · · · · · · · · ·

◆ MANAGING TIME ◆

It can be useful to set an alarm on a clock or on your phone for however long you intend to meditate. There are also many apps that you can use to sound a bell when your allocated mindfulness minutes are up.

▲ ▲ ▲

CREATING SPACE FOR MINDFUL PRACTICE

You don't need any special equipment to be mindful. It's a myth that you need to sit cross-legged on the floor, or buy special cushions and meditation stools. You definitely do not need an entire meditation room at your disposal. You just need yourself and somewhere comfortable: a chair, sofa, corner or space to sit and practise. It doesn't need to be any more complicated than that.

FINDING THE RIGHT POSTURE FOR YOU

If you are meditating for long periods of time, there are some postural guidelines that you might want to consider. You can sit on a chair, on the floor, on a stool or a sofa.

If you are sitting, we often talk about an upright, dignified posture. This means that you are not leaning back or leaning to the side on a chair arm.

If you do this and close your eyes, your brain might slip into sleep mode and you'll find yourself dozing off. You'll find an upright posture is helpful to remain awake. Keep your back as straight as you can without it being uncomfortable. If you find cushions helpful to support your back, grab some before you start.

Your eyes can be open or closed or held in a soft gaze towards a single point in front of you. You're not looking at anything specifically – just keeping your gaze steady without attempting to focus on what's there. Tuck your chin in a little and lower your gaze slightly if your eyes are open.

Place your arms by the side of your upper body. Your hands can be placed upon your thighs or knees in a position that's comfortable for you.

Cushions and a blanket can be useful additions to support you and keep you warm when you meditate. Remember to modify and adapt your posture as and when you need to, ensuring that you are comfortable. Being kind to yourself is part of your practice.

LETTING GO AND DROPPING INTO MINDFULNESS

Most of the time we live in our heads. We constantly think, do and plan, day in and day out. Mindfulness provides us with the opportunity to create another way of being. While we're inhabiting that space in our heads, we're largely unaware of what we are feeling in our body. Letting go of the thoughts buzzing around our mind and dropping into what's happening in your body allows you to return to your physical senses. You can reconnect to embodied emotions. Try this 'letting go' exercise.

· · · · · · · · · · · ● · ● · ● ● ● · ● · ● · · · · · · · · ·

Letting go

Time: five minutes

Begin by finding a comfortable posture. Close your eyes or adopt a soft gaze. Slowly shift your focus to your breathing. Notice the sensations of each breath as you inhale and exhale. Allow your attention to settle here, in the breath.

· · · · ●

Gently direct your attention towards your body. Mindfully tune in to the different sensations. What do you notice? What's here? Continuing to breathe normally, see if it's possible to focus on your head. Bring your attention in turn to your mouth, your eyes, your nose, your temples, your forehead. How does it feel? What sensations are you able to detect? Really notice what's here. Take three breaths. Let go and move on.

● · · · ·

Now let your attention move towards your shoulders. Bring your curiosity to this area. You're not judging or trying to change what's here. Investigate each sensation with kindness. Is it possible to name the sensations? Now take three breaths. Let go and move on.

· · · ● ●

Shifting the focus of your attention to the back now, what do you observe? Notice the upper back, the middle of the back and the lower back. Moving from the back to the abdomen with the same gentle curiosity. What's here? Take three breaths. Let go and move on.

● ● ● ● ·

Next, bring your focus to the lower body. Your bottom, thighs, calves and feet. Is your body holding onto tension? Be specific as you consider each area, noticing what is here without trying to change it. Take three breaths. Let go.

· · ● ● ●

Return to the sensations of each breath. After three breaths, gently stop the practice.

Remember, there is no goal with mindfulness. You're not trying to achieve anything, so you can't 'do it wrong'. Sometimes, when we first start meditating, it's easy for your mind to wander, to become distracted and think that you just can't do it. That's a little harsh! We need to remember that mindfulness isn't a race or a competition. Just sitting down and doing it is enough.

▲▲▲

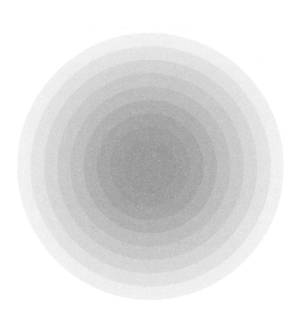

LIVING
in the present
MOMENT

◆ DON'T WAIT TO GET HAPPY ◆

What makes us happy? Probably not what you think. Rather than chasing happiness, or waiting for it to come to us, the answer is more surprising. Researcher Matt Killingsworth discovered that we are at our happiest when we are in the present moment. This held true even when people were doing something that they found unpleasant. Our unhappiest moments are when our minds are wandering. Put more simply, we are at our happiest when we are being mindful.

◆ THE THREE ARROWS ◆

The Buddhist parable of the three arrows can be useful in examining how we mindfully approach negative events.

▶

The first arrow is the negative event. This is the bad thing that has happened which can cause us pain, stress or anxiety.

▶ ▶

The second arrow is our reaction to the negative event. This is our anger or sadness or complaining about the event. It's the self-blame and beating ourselves up when things go wrong. Perhaps asking yourself, 'Why me?'

▶ ▶ ▶

The third arrow is how we keep revisiting and ruminating on the event. When we turn it over and over in our mind, we create more pain for ourselves.

The lesson of the three arrows? It's how we choose to respond to the events that come our way that shapes our experience. Becoming more mindful helps us to recognize the second arrow when it arises before we are in the grip of self-blame. We can learn to be kinder to ourselves, to exercise self-compassion when things go wrong. Noticing these habitual thought patterns can help us to become unstuck from negative cycles of thinking that affect our overall happiness.

POSITIVE PSYCHOLOGY: A NEW PARADIGM

Traditionally, psychology has looked at what is wrong with human beings. A model that examines what isn't working rather than what is. Positive psychology offers a different perspective. This new school of psychology looks at what is happening when people are thriving, when they are at their happiest. It's a different way of looking at the world and one that mindfulness sits comfortably within. Being more mindful in your life choices can improve your level of happiness. Mindfulness is often used by positive psychologists to build self-awareness, self-regulation and self-compassion.

MINDFULNESS AND DIGITAL DOWNTIME

Technology is amazing: it provides us with a vehicle to do all manner of life-enhancing things, from learning new information to maintaining social connections, but it has a downside. Have you ever noticed that you are constantly connected to technology? If you frequently refresh your feed, email late into the night or scroll through social media for longer than you intended, you might be experiencing some of the less positive aspects of technology. On its own, technology isn't inherently negative but, for some of us, it might be time to unplug (at least for a while).

Why do we feel so drawn to the online world? It's all down to a part of the brain known as the ventral tegmental area (VTA). Each time you get a like or a message on social media, a hit of dopamine is released creating feelings of pleasure and reward. It's no wonder we can't put our devices down. Digital addiction is harmful to our health, compromising our immune system and our wellbeing.

FOMO (fear of missing out), or thinking that others are having more fun than we are, can also be harmful. People's social media feeds are carefully curated, and often bear little relation to reality. The inevitable comparisons that we make lead to a decrease in self-esteem and an increase in low mood. Studies have shown that time spent on social media has been linked to an increase in depression. If you find yourself spending long periods of time online, it's worth thinking about consciously managing your digital world, becoming more mindful about where and when you use it.

Mindful practices to create digital downtime

Decide upon the amount of time that you want to spend online and stick to it. You can set an alert or install an app that will tell you when time's up. This is a really effective way to bring mindfulness to your digital use. In the same way that you set an intention before meditating, you can set an intention before you go online.

Consider unplugging for one day a week. Bringing mindfulness to your digital habits will help you to be more intentional in your use of technology. This will also enable you to monitor the amount of time that you spend mindlessly online. Think of it as a digital detox.

Disable alerts on your device for news and apps. Without the distraction of alerts popping up on your screen, you'll find it easier to manage your interaction with technology.

Bring a curiosity to your online use by implementing a mindful traffic light system. Notice which sites, contacts and sources of information leave you feeling energized and positive. These are green light sites that will enhance your day. Are there sites that occasionally result in you experiencing low mood afterwards? These sites are allocated an amber light. Slow down and proceed with caution – monitor your use. Sites, online contacts or apps that leave you feeling depressed, stressed or anxious are red light sites and to be avoided.

Bulletproofing yourself against the news

In times of stress, continuous checking of the news might temporarily make us feel more in control. What mindless consumption of news will actually do is push us into stress mode. While facts can reduce fear, they need to come from a credible source. The uninterrupted consumption of news from multiple sources can feel overwhelming. Your brain on this kind of news is like Velcro. It will latch onto anything negative because that's the way that we're built: it's our negativity bias in action. Anything positive, unfortunately, is like Teflon – it won't stick. This is where mindful consumption of news can be invaluable.

Practices to limit news overwhelm

Decide how often each day you will check news sites and stick to your allocated time. Do not engage in 'mission creep', where you jump from one site to another on autopilot.

Identify credible news sources and rely on those for your information. Don't get sucked into reading and watching news from unverified sources that are likely to ramp up your stress levels, leading to anxiety.

CREATING A
HAPPINESS DEFAULT

It's possible to create a happiness default by really paying attention to where you place your focus when you encounter different types of media. Consider your consumption of the following:

- Television

- Music

- Podcasts

- Radio

- Movies

- Newspapers

- Online forums

Keep a journal of how you feel when you engage with each of these areas. Do you notice any themes or patterns emerging with particular choices? Consider spending more time on areas that lift and energize you.

WATERING THE SEEDS OF HAPPINESS

What we focus on expands. It makes sense then, if we are living mindfully, that we focus our attention on areas that nourish us. Be selective about which seeds you water (the things that you pay attention to). Happiness doesn't mean that we won't suffer; we will, and that's part of life. We cannot avoid it. We only have a choice in how we respond to that suffering (remember the three arrows, page 50). Buddhist monk Thích Nhất Hạnh describes this as 'inviting positive seeds', and watering them. We can do this by selectively paying attention to the positive things around and within us. This is an effective way of watering the seeds of happiness.

Each day, choose three positive seeds in your life that you would like to mindfully nourish and water.

▲▲▲

MINDFULNESS
&
COMPASSION

◆ BEING KIND TO YOURSELF ◆

Sometimes, our inner narrative can be less than kind. That little voice that chats away telling you that you're not good enough: 'You're a failure', 'You're always...', 'You should...'

That voice is there for most of us. For some people it's constant, for others it's every now and again. See if it's possible to monitor your self-talk for twenty-four hours. What do you notice? Pretty unkind, isn't it?

Being kind to ourselves is mostly something that we have to learn. Kristin Neff, one of the world's leading compassion researchers, describes self-compassion as:

> 'Treating yourself with the same kindness, concern and support you'd show to a good friend. When faced with difficult life struggles, or confronting personal mistakes, failures, and inadequacies, self-compassion responds with kindness rather than harsh self-judgement.'

➤ REFRAME YOUR SELF-TALK ➤

Monitor your self-talk and see if it's possible to reframe any negative narrative that you spot. Instead of, 'I did something really dumb,' try, 'I've learned from that experience and I'll make different choices next time.'

➤ DEVELOP POSITIVE SELF-TALK ➤

This isn't about pretending that everything is perfect when it isn't. Think of positive self-talk as your own internal cheerleader. This will prevent your fear-based, negative dialogue from taking over. Create some positive phrases that resonate with you that you can draw upon during difficult times.

This is temporary.

· · · • •

*I've overcome situations like
this before, I can do this.*

• • · · ·

If I don't try, I've failed anyway.

◆ GIVE YOURSELF A HUG ◆

When we receive a hug (even from ourselves) it releases the feel-good hormone oxytocin. When you feel stressed, wrap your arms around yourself and give yourself a hug. Notice how it feels as you hold yourself.

◆ THE SCIENCE OF COMPASSION ◆

Researchers have found that compassion is strongly related to our wellbeing and resilience. When we're kinder to ourselves, it becomes easier to manage difficulties. Practising self-compassion has been linked to decreased anxiety, reduced depression, less reactive behaviour and a reduction in our self-limiting beliefs. When we are mindful of our difficulties with life's challenges we can respond with compassion and kindness, developing an inner strength that enables us to thrive.

▲▲▲

◆ RESISTANCE TO COMPASSION ◆

Sometimes, we hold on to internal barriers when it comes to self-compassion. We don't believe that we deserve it, or perhaps we think that we're being self-indulgent. Maybe you recognize, as you read this, that you sometimes resort to self-blaming or self-shaming, otherwise known as self-sabotage. Often when people first begin practising self-compassion, they experience what's known as 'compassion backdraft'.

When we direct mindfulness to areas that we've previously ignored or avoided, it's as though we are illuminating a corner of darkness. It can easily start to feel as though those areas are being amplified. That's compassion backdraft.

When you notice a backdraft arising, be gentle with yourself. It's okay to stop, or pause, and take a self-compassion break. There's no need to attempt to push through it. Do whatever you need to do to reduce those feelings. Get some fresh air, go out in nature, sit in the sunshine, listen to music – all of those small acts of kindness can become part of your self-compassion routine. Instead of blaming yourself, you're creating a new relationship, a more helpful way of interacting with your imperfections.

◆ IF I WAS A FRIEND ◆

When you are faced with a difficult situation, ask yourself: 'How would I treat a friend?' Aim to treat yourself as though you were a close, dear and valued friend who you want to support.

. . . . ● ● ● ● ● ● . . . .

Self-compassion pause

You can use this practice either in difficult situations or when you recall a past event that is causing you stress.

Is it possible to mindfully explore the event? Can you detect any physical or emotional discomfort in your body?

Pause. Take a breath. Say to yourself:

· · · · ● ●

This is a moment of discomfort.

● ● · · ·

Discomfort and suffering are part of life. I'm not alone. Other people also feel this way.

· · · ● ●

May I be kind to myself.

● ● · · ·

How can I provide kindness and compassion to myself in this moment?

· · · ● ●

There may be other phrases that also work for you in this moment. Use this whenever you need self-support.

◆ SELF-CARE AND MINDFULNESS ◆

Self-care is another way of practising mindful self-compassion. Self-care includes anything that you do to take care of your physical, emotional or mental health. Scheduling time for yourself is important. Self-care techniques have been found to lower stress and increase self-esteem. It's easy to forget to take care of yourself when you get caught up in other commitments. Self-care can include:

- eating nutritious food

- reducing your stress levels

- time alone

- yoga

- stretching

- time in nature

- creating an opportunity for physical exercise.

Conscious breathing

This is a useful technique when you are in the grip of stress or anxiety and need to exercise self-compassion. Take a few deliberate, deep, slow breaths and then repeat. It's one of the fastest ways to reduce the physiological symptoms of stress.

A SLEEP-LOSS EPIDEMIC AND MINDFULNESS

The World Health Organization has declared that we are experiencing a sleep-loss epidemic. Lack of sleep can contribute to the risk of heart disease, cancer and Alzheimer's disease. Sleep scientists have discovered that mindfulness is an effective treatment for adults with chronic insomnia. Bringing mindfulness to your bedtime routine is an opportunity to practise self-care and create an effective sleep strategy.

Take a mindful look at your sleep hygiene: are there things that you do before sleep (using devices, watching TV) that are unhelpful? Develop a pre-sleep routine that relaxes you before bedtime. Steps could include:

- Keeping your bedroom device-free

- Laying off caffeine six hours before sleep

- Creating a cool, dark space in which to wind down

- Listening to a guided meditation before sleep

- Doing the body scan (see page 37)

- Tensing and relaxing each part of your body in turn.

▲▲▲

CALMING
anxiety with
MINDFULNESS

LOSING CONTROL: WHAT'S REALLY GOING ON

Remember the amygdala? That's the part of the brain that determines our emotional response to any given situation. It registers input (what is happening) as pleasurable or threatening. All well and good it if registers a pleasurable response, but when it registers a threat, 'fight, flight or freeze' begins to kick in. That response evolved to protect us, and often it does, but sometimes it can be problematic, mistaking anxiety for real threats.

The amygdala is the least effective part of our brain for thinking clearly and rationally. Imagine your brain as a house on three levels: the amygdala is the basement. It cannot differentiate between real, imminent threats and perceived threats, which may be a false alarm. That fake threat can trigger problematic reactive behaviour.

For example, imagine that you are asked to do some public speaking: you might avoid the situation altogether (flight response) or find yourself lost for words (freeze response). Another stressful situation could occur during an argument that becomes heated and one person shouts (fight response). None of these events would be life-threatening, yet our brain becomes unable to think clearly when they happen. Impulse and reactivity take over, and that's when we do and say things that we later regret. It's the basement in the house taking over again, as the amygdala reduces our capacity to access, store and recall information that might help us.

A regular mindfulness practice helps to reduce the activity in the amygdala, enabling us to connect to our clear-thinking prefrontal cortex (PFC). It's no wonder the PFC is often referred to as the control centre of the brain. It helps us to focus, access calming strategies, communicate effectively, regulate our emotions and exercise empathy – placing us in a much better position to respond, rather than reacting unhelpfully to whatever is going on.

▲ ▲ ▲

◆ IDENTIFY TRIGGERS ◆

Mindfully investigate your anxiety triggers. Once you can recognize them you can begin to manage or limit your exposure. When you see that a trigger is emerging it can be helpful to try active relaxation, for example going for a walk.

MINDFULNESS AND NATURE: CREATING CALM

There's a huge amount of data around the benefits of spending time in nature. When we're out in green space it has the effect of soothing and calming our mind and our body. The natural world provides renewal for us. Researchers have even found that just by looking at images of nature we are able to reduce our stress levels. Spending even a little time in nature, for example taking a walk outside on a lunch break, or sitting in a garden, is an effective way to reduce overall stress and manage anxiety.

▲▲▲

Developing mindfulness in nature

Bring your focus to your current state, either as you arrive in a green space or before you go. How are you feeling? What do you notice? Are you relaxed or stressed?

Sit in silence and notice the sounds and sights around you. Is it possible to hear birds singing? Are you able to feel the warmth of the sun of your face? Is there a breeze? Perhaps you notice the buzzing of bees as they move among the flowers. Take in everything around you as you sit.

After ten minutes revisit that check-in from the start. What do you notice? How do you feel? What is your mood right now, as you sit in this natural space?

MINDFULNESS TECHNIQUES TO TAME YOUR INNER CRITIC

The inner critic is the voice that comments on everything from your appearance to what other people are thinking about you (none of it is positive). That voice is a bit of a bully and is a critical component of anxiety. It can crush your confidence, but it doesn't have to.

- - - - - - - - - - - - ● ● ● ● ● ● - - - - - - - - - -

Even breaths

Bring your focus to your breath. Relax your shoulders. Aim to achieve an even in-breath and an even out-breath. Continue even breaths until you feel your physiological response to anxiety start to subside.

Journal

An effective way to deactivate your negative self-talk is to keep a journal. Learn to identify the voice when you hear it and keep a record of each statement. In one column, list all of the negative things that you hear. Then, create a second column and talk back to your inner critic. Write down all of the reasons it is wrong.

STOP FEELING BAD ABOUT FEELING BAD

Feeling bad about feeling bad is one of our least helpful habits as human beings. Telling ourselves that we shouldn't feel what we are feeling heaps guilt on top of already difficult emotions. Resisting what we feel in the hope of avoiding negative emotions is counterproductive. Times of difficulty and feeling bad are part of life. Just as we are sometimes happy, we will also experience sadness. It's all part of the human condition. These feelings are known as 'meta-emotions' (emotions we feel in response to another emotion).

Our emotions provide us with valuable information. Our brain has evolved to keep us safe. When we feel bad, we can mindfully examine what's going on. Is it a response that we can act upon to remain safe, or is it an unhelpful fear based emotion? When we mindfully examine our emotions in this way, we can learn to tell the difference between negative thoughts that are helpful and those which are not. We can then make an informed choice about how to respond.

DIALECTICAL BEHAVIOUR THERAPY

Known as Dialectical Behaviour Therapy (DBT), this technique helps you to manage your emotions. It is a way of identifying and mindfully labelling your emotions so that you can manage them. Ask:

◀ *What is that feeling?* ▶

◀ *Is it sadness?* ▶

◀ *Helplessness?* ▶

◄ *Anger?* ►

◄ *What else?* ►

Once you've named it, see if it's possible to explore where in your mind or your body you are feeling it. Are your fists clenched? Are your shoulders tense? Do you notice an increased heart rate?

MAKING FRIENDS WITH YOUR DIFFICULT FEELINGS

When we mindfully identify our emotions on a regular basis, we come to recognize that thoughts are not facts. Your relationship with your thoughts can become neutral, neither positive nor negative. When you adopt this stance, you are no longer defined by your thoughts.

▲▲▲

HOW TO DEAL WITH NEGATIVE EMOTIONS

We can learn how to control our emotions to ensure that they don't end up controlling us. Pretending that negative emotions aren't there doesn't work. It won't make them disappear. What we avoid, persists, and can result in maladaptive coping strategies, such as misusing food or alcohol. What we don't acknowledge eventually becomes even harder to manage.

The ability to deal with emotions is known as self-regulation or impulse control. Think of self-regulation as happening in two stages. The first stage, self-awareness, is bringing your attention to your thoughts, and recognizing your emotions as they arise. This is a skill that can be developed. Stage two is dealing with them in a skilful way rather than responding with a knee-jerk reaction. The key to self-regulation is practice.

▲ ▲ ▲

→ AFFECT LABELLING ←

Affect labelling is a mindful practice that is used to identify emotions. Identifying your difficult emotions helps us to control them.

Take a deep breath and without judgement, examine the emotions present for you right now.

What do you notice? Is there one emotion, or more?

When emotions are difficult there can be a fine granularity to them. Are you angry? Sad? Frustrated? Do you feel shame or embarrassment?

As you begin to employ affect labelling you'll get better at identifying your emotions as they arise. Then you can begin to create distance between those emotions and how you choose to respond to them.

→ REFRAME YOUR THOUGHTS ←

We all look at the world through a personal filter. That filter depends upon a number of variables from how we were raised, our experiences throughout life to how we are feeling today, in this moment. When we feel stressed or anxious, we automatically perceive the world as more threatening and dangerous.

When you notice your negative thoughts, pause. Is it possible to reframe that thought? Is there another way of looking at it? For example, you might think to yourself, 'There's no point in trying to exercise. I'm useless at physical activity.' A way of reframing this might be, 'I'll start slowly and build from there. No one is perfect at anything the first time they try. My fitness will improve with time.'

USING MINDFULNESS TO CURATE YOUR STRESS RESPONSE

Each of these quick techniques will relax your nervous system by around 5 per cent each time that you do them. To really experience their benefits, the key is repetition. Incorporate them into your daily routine.

Counting-breath meditation

This is a way of developing present-moment awareness. It's a deceptively simple technique that will help you to quickly reduce your physiological response to stress during difficult moments.

As you breathe in, count 1, 2, 3, 4, 5 and then, before you breathe out, pause for one second.

Now exhale and count 1, 2, 3, 4, 5 and pause for a second again.

Now inhale and repeat the process.

By concentrating your focus on your breath, you will begin to calm your mind and your body. You can use this practice for as little as sixty seconds, or longer if you wish to.

The 4 - 6 - 8 breath

The 4 - 6 - 8 breath can be done in a short space of time. This practice will move the activity from your limbic system, the part of your brain responsible for your behavioural and emotional response, to your prefrontal cortex (PFC) (see page 71). The PFC, responsible for executive functioning, sends your body the message, 'In this moment, I am okay.'

Breathe in for four seconds. Hold your breath for six seconds, or as long as is comfortable for you. Exhale for eight seconds. Repeat.

The purpose of this practice is to relax your nervous system.

Grounding your body

Another really effective way to reduce stress and anxiety in the moment is to become physiologically grounded. Scanning your body, ask:

◀ *Can I feel my feet?* ▶

◀ *Can I feel my legs?* ▶

◀ *Can I feel my lower abdomen?* ▶

◀ *My heart?* ▶

How about your arms?
◀ *Your hands? Your shoulders? Your head?* ▶
Your face? Lips, cheeks, eyes?

By grounding yourself in this way, you'll be shifting blood flow away from the limbic system and soothing yourself.

Think of ways that you can creatively build these short practices into your day.

· · · · · · · · · · · ● ● ● ● ● ● ● ● ● ● · · · · · · ·

▲▲▲

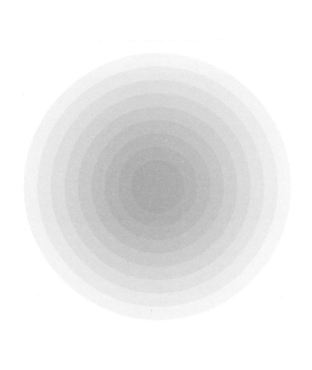

MINDFULNESS

at

WORK

◆ THE BURNOUT EPIDEMIC ◆

We are in the middle of what the World Health Organization has described as a burnout epidemic. Workplace burnout was recently recognized by the WHO as an occupational phenomenon specifically caused by chronic workplace stress. Burnout is characterized by emotional exhaustion, cynicism and ineffectiveness at work. Often the organizational culture that we work in contributes to our burnout. Working long hours, emailing late into the night, the inability to switch off and constant connection all contribute to burnout. This is the least effective way of working for sustainable performance. It's a dynamic that needs to be addressed by organizations, leaders and individuals together.

◆ PRESSURE, STRESS AND FLOW ◆

How much stress is too much? You might be surprised to know that stress isn't all bad. We need some form of pressure to motivate us, to stave off boredom. This is known as 'eustress' and we need it. As the pressure builds we move towards our optimum performance, or 'flow', as it is known by scientists.

Flow is characterized by being completely focused on the task at hand, losing track of time and feeling stretched in terms of what we are working on (it isn't easy). As things become progressively more difficult we tip over into stress.

Our bodies are designed to be able to this. We can usually dip in and out of stress without difficulty. It's when we tip over from flow into stress and stay there for long periods of time that we begin to burn out and ill health ensues. So how do we prevent burnout from happening?

BUILDING RESILIENCE BRICK BY BRICK WITH MINDFULNESS

It's possible to create a series of really quick wins in building resilience at work by looking at how you manage your day. Using mindfulness, we can begin to notice where our energy is depleted and where it is renewed. Habits such as skipping breakfast or eating lunch at our desk all feed into the onset of stress and burnout. When we try to push through stressful periods by not having breaks or taking work home we actually become less effective, not more.

Known as 'sacrifice syndrome', this usually starts at the top of an organization and slowly permeates the culture, becoming the accepted norm. Sacrifice syndrome only ever leads to burnout, so when you spot it, it's important to tackle it.

◆ THE MYTH OF MULTITASKING ◆

Multitasking is a myth. What's really happening when we focus on more than one thing at a time is that our error rate increases. Every time we move from one task to another, known as switch-tasking, we increase our cognitive load and that increases our stress. Mapping your energy throughout the day can help you to more productively schedule your tasks.

WORK WITH YOUR CIRCADIAN RHYTHM

Grade your tasks into low-, medium- or high-focus. Order them together into low-cognitive-load, medium-load and high-load blocks. Try to work out the time of day when your focus and energy are at their peak. This is the time for those high-focus, high-load, more complex tasks. Then, identify any dips in your energy and schedule in the low-focus tasks (or breaks) that aren't going to drain you.

ATTENTION-DEFICIT CULTURES

We sometimes work in organizations that demonstrate what Edward Hallowell, MD, describes as an 'attentional deficit trait culture'. By that, he means that some places of work have evolved to become places of constant distraction. Multiple interruptions, unmanageable demands on time and constant connection make it virtually impossible to achieve flow, while adding to your cognitive load. Even when you are working from home, you might recognize this pattern of working. Your attention can be pulled in multiple directions, making focus less than easy.

You can bring mindfulness to your place of work, wherever that might be, by dialling down those continuous interruptions. You can create a different way of working by optimizing your performance with mindfulness.

- -

Energy audit

Audit your day to see how your work practices may affect your energy levels. Ask yourself:

- What energizes me?

- What depletes me?

- Am I creating downtime?

- Are there regular pauses in my day – especially after stressful periods?

Adopt periodization, a technique used in sports psychology to plan your day. This means that when you experience periods of intense, complex activity they are followed by downtime. This will prevent sacrifice syndrome and help you build more renewal into your day, increasing your resilience.

OPTIMIZING YOUR PERFORMANCE

Mindfulness enables us to optimize our performance by training our focus. Whether engaging in formal or informal practice, consistent repetition over time will improve our memory and our focus on any given task. It also optimizes our performance when we work with other people, by developing our emotional intelligence.

▲▲▲

◆ EMOTIONAL INTELLIGENCE ◆

Emotional intelligence is a crucial differentiator in the workplace. It's the ability to recognize and regulate your own emotions, as well as the emotions of people around you. It's about knowing what you are feeling, as you are feeling it, and being able to manage it skilfully.

Rather than something you either have or you don't, emotional intelligence is comprised of a profile of competencies including motivation, self-regulation, self-awareness and empathy. It's also something that we can learn to develop with a regular mindfulness practice. We can only manage what we are able to bring awareness to, and that's where mindfulness comes in.

◆ REDUCING YOUR ◆ COGNITIVE LOAD

When our cognitive load is high and we're stressed, usually the first thing that evaporates is our self-regulation. Stress often leads to a short fuse. Reflect upon the last time that you were stressed – how did it impact your ability to manage your emotions? By reducing your cognitive load, it's possible to lower the pressure on your limbic system. You can do this by practising self-care throughout the day: taking regular breaks, hydrating, and maintaining steady glucose levels.

◆ MONO-TASKING ◆

Mono-tasking is the opposite of multitasking. It involves focusing on one task at a time. Plan your day mindfully, so that if you have a high-focus task you are minimizing interruptions.

◆ STOP SWITCH-TASKING ◆

This is really about retraining your brain. To begin with, monitor how many times you switch from one task to another. You might be surprised as this is often done on autopilot. Designate half-hour segments to each batch of compartmentalized tasks. If you're struggling, use an alarm, an app or egg timer and don't budge until times up.

COMPASSION AND KINDNESS ◆ AS A KEY DIFFERENTIATOR ◆ AT WORK – YES, REALLY

Compassion and work may seem like strange bedfellows, but there is a growing body of research that suggests compassion at work creates an environment where people flourish. When we're happy at work, our productivity, performance and motivation increase. We feel better and we do better when our emotional needs are met.

It isn't about being a soft touch, or feeling sorry for someone. Think of compassion as noticing someone's suffering, combined with empathy and the motivation to help. When we view compassion this way, you'll begin to see that there are many opportunities to practise compassion at work.

Compassion has been linked to improved performance that results in a competitive advantage. We've looked at the burnout epidemic and how stress at work can have a negative impact upon performance. Compassionate workplaces have begun to address this, looking for ways to mitigate against it.

When organizations respond compassionately to their staff (and to each other) psychological safety increases. We are better placed to learn and sustain our performance. Businesses that recognize this foster a culture where people are more willing to admit mistakes, to learn from them, and to be more collaborative when it comes to problem-solving.

It's possible to mindfully bring more compassion into your work by:

- Paying attention to your colleagues. Bring mindfulness to your interactions so that you are able to notice when someone needs help. If you're in a meeting or a conversation, don't use your phone at the same time.

- Demonstrate empathy towards your colleagues (even the ones that you may not like very much). Build relationships by being present and offering to help people.

- Publicly recognize and reward compassionate behaviour.

- Adopt a growth mindset by making it part of your culture to talk about mistakes and what you have learned from them.

- If you lead an organization or a team, model a growth mindset and tell them how you personally have learned from failure.

◆ CREATING A MORE MINDFUL WORKPLACE ◆

Researchers have found that workplace mindfulness programmes result in reduced levels of stress and burnout along with improved focus, greater productivity, more creativity and improved decision-making.

When we work in a culture of constant distraction it can be exhausting. But what does a mindful workplace look like, and how do you create it? A mindful workplace is less frenetic. It creates time for pauses, and works with intention. To create a mindful workplace:

- Begin your day with intention. How do you want to work? Consider creating a schedule that supports mindfulness rather than constantly rushing around.

- Mono-task and reduce distractions. Create flow opportunities by carving out periods of the day for high-focus. If it's possible, designate a quiet space, where people are able to work in flow without interruptions.

- Build in time to reflect upon how you're working and whether it is effective for you.

- Introduce moments in the day when you shift from doing to being. Press pause and notice how you feel, right here, right now – with

no agenda other than to check in and build
awareness of your present state.

- Mindfully walk between meetings, up stairs
  and along corridors. This is an excellent way
  to build mindful movement into your day,
  while at the same time grounding yourself
  physically.

- Tempted to respond to a cranky email with
  like-for-like? Stop. Take a breath. Bring your
  awareness to whatever you are experiencing
  without judging it. Notice emotions, feelings
  and physical sensations as they arise. Is there
  tightness in your stomach? Are your fists
  clenched? Your shoulders tense? Breathe
  again and then step away. Develop your
  emotional intelligence by learning to pause
  and reflect before you respond.

▲▲▲

MINDFULNESS

for when

YOU'RE TOO BUSY

A perceived lack of time can prevent many of us from practising mindfulness. Informally building mindfulness into your day, using everyday tasks as mindful anchors, is a way of relieving that time pressure.

◆ CREATING OPPORTUNITIES TO WAKE UP ◆

Think of these informal moments of mindfulness as an opportunity to wake up and disrupt autopilot. When you are caught up in the 'doing' of the day, you can choose, instead, to create moments of 'being'.

Three meditations you can do right now

1. One way of bringing ourselves back into the present moment is to mindfully listen to the sounds around you. Are they loud or quiet?

Near or far? Do you notice that you enjoy some sounds more than others? Focus on the rich tapestry of sounds surrounding you that you might otherwise ignore.

2. Stop and name five things that you can see, hear and feel.

3. Mindfully tense and release your body. Bring your focus to the physical sensations of tensing. Notice the difference. Clench your fists, feel your nails against your hands. Pay attention to how it feels. Do this for ten seconds every hour – set a regular alert to remind you.

Applying mindfulness to mundane activities

Start small by choosing one or two keystone habits daily, routine activities that you can bring mindfulness to. You can add to your routine as you become more confident and more curious.

- **Public transport.** If you have habits of transportation, do your best to disrupt them. Deliberately sit in a different seat on the bus, train or underground. Get off a stop early and walk the remainder of your journey.

- **Making your bed.** Instead of throwing the duvet back over the bed, bring your focus to the fabric, the colour, texture and temperature of it. Straighten your pillows, noticing the softness and bounce as they spring back from your touch.

- **Washing.** How does the water feel against your skin? Do you notice sensations of pleasure at the warmth, or invigoration if the temperature is cooler? Notice your reaction to soap or shower gel. Is it gloopy, or thin? How does it smell? Feel the consistency of it against your skin. The way the soap changes texture as it meets water and suds begin to appear. Bring present moment awareness to your energy levels before and after washing. Do you feel revitalized? Relaxed?

◆ MINDFUL DRIVING ◆

Driving can be a hugely stressful experience, while at the same time presenting an opportunity to be mindful. This is one practice where you definitely shouldn't close your eyes. Instead, when you reach traffic lights or a stop sign, bring your awareness to how you are feeling. Are you stressed? Is your grip on the steering wheel tight? Are you relaxed? Angry? Frustrated? Late? Notice and then breathe in for a count of four, hold your breath for six and exhale for eight.

◆ PLEASANT/UNPLEASANT ◆

Bring your attention to your preferences. With openness and curiosity, notice the physical and emotional sensations around you. Are you able to identify pleasant, unpleasant or neutral preferences? Without judging, gently acknowledge what you notice.

▲ ▲ ▲

◆ MINDFUL WALKING ◆

Wherever you're walking – along a corridor between meetings, along the pavement or in the park, really bring your attention to your surroundings. What can you see? Focus on the sounds around you, the aroma, the light as it bounces off surfaces, the colours that surround you. Notice how your body feels. The way your core is centred by moving each leg. What are the physical movements that walking reveals to you?

◆ MINDFUL MOVEMENT ◆

Think about how you might build mindful stretches into your day. If you're working at a laptop or device, create moments where you step away from it. Lift your arms above your head, press your arms down towards your sides, move from foot to foot to energize yourself, and focus on how your body feels as you move around.

▲▲▲

◆ MINDFUL EATING ◆

Do you sometimes find yourself eating while doing something else – watching TV, working on something else or checking your phone? Eating has almost become something that we don't have time for unless we are pairing it with something else.

Mindful eating is one of the easiest ways of bringing yourself back to being during the day. Minimize distractions when you sit down to eat. Turn off your phone and place your attention on your feelings of hunger.

Focus on your food: the texture, the colour, the aroma, the temperature. Become aware of your energy levels before and after you eat.

Research shows that eating mindfully helps us to regulate our intake as well as improving digestion. See if it's possible to pay attention to when you are really full, when you've had enough. If you choose to, use this to end your meal when you are ready instead of habitually finishing what is in front of you.

▲▲▲

CREATING A
sustainable
MINDFUL LIFE

Congratulations, you've started your mindfulness journey. It's a practice that will sustain you throughout your life. So how are you going to sustain your practice? Exercise some self-compassion and be kind to yourself. Even sixty seconds a day is better than nothing. If there are days that you don't practise, well, that's okay too. Think of mindfulness as a marathon rather than a sprint. You'll get there in the end.

◆ HABIT ENERGY, HABIT LOOPS ◆ AND MINDFUL CHANGE

Habits take time to build. Researchers at MIT have discovered that every habit is formed of three components:

- Cue – this alerts us to choose a particular activity from all of the stored routines that we possess.

- Routine – our routine follows the cue. For

example, we wake up, turn off our alarm and scroll through new emails.

- Reward – the positive reinforcement we get from our action. If we're checking our emails, it might be a hit of dopamine as we feel that we're attending to what the day brings. It might also be causing stress, but we're less likely to notice that if we're hooked into the habit.

You've probably noticed by now, as you become more mindful, that some habits serve us well, while others don't. That's one of the many reasons for deciding to make mindfulness part of your life. Use the habit loop formula to identify your cue for this, for example:

● ● ● · ·

When I wake up (cue) I will practise mindful breathing for five minutes (routine) because I want to set an intention to be more mindful as I begin my day (reward).

· · · ● ●

Wherever you want to build a mindfulness habit, identify your reasons and create a plan. Research suggests that when you write your goal down, you're more likely to stick to it. Try creating your own example.

When _____ *(cue), I will* _____ *(routine)*
because it provides me with _____ *(reward).*

◆ MINDFULNESS AND CHANGE ◆

Mindfulness can help you to implement and navigate change more skilfully. Change that we choose can energize us and have a positive impact. Change that we don't choose can arrive with uncertainty and anxiety. Life involves change, we can't stop it. When we resist change or try to avoid it, we create unhelpful emotions, adding to our load. Mindfulness can help us to adopt a more proactive approach. When we use mindfulness to lean into and accept the uncertainties of life, we are better placed to respond to them.

Change is universal. Accept that it will happen. Adopting mindful acceptance doesn't mean that you become passive. By being more mindful, you won't waste time resisting or avoiding change. Instead, you'll be equipped to look at the components of change and manage it more effectively. Ask yourself:

- What am I feeling?

- What are my thoughts around this change?

- How are those thoughts affecting me?

- What does this change mean for me?

- How can I adapt?

- What is the best way forward for me?

- How can I plan my next steps?

Even though mindfulness won't prevent change it will help you to avoid overwhelm. You'll minimize knee-jerk amygdala reactions and be able to move forward more effectively.

CULTIVATING JOY WITH MINDFULNESS

Sometimes we're so focused on reducing stress and increasing resilience with mindfulness, that we forget about joy. In the same way that we are able to develop our mindfulness, we can also cultivate joy by practising more of it.

See if it's possible to create awe in everyday things that you might otherwise ignore. You could be playing with a pet, talking to a good friend, meditating in your garden first thing, creating a morning coffee ritual or watching the sun stream in through a window. Train yourself to pay attention to these small things, discovering your own unique joy triggers.

Loving-kindness meditation

Focusing on self-compassion will help you to access your inner joy. Practising a loving-kindness meditation (also known as 'metta' meditation) will help you to develop compassion and stop comparing yourself to other people, becoming kinder to yourself and others. Silently repeat to yourself:

● ● · · ·

May I be filled with loving kindness.
May I be well. May I be peaceful. May I be loved.
May I be truly happy.

· · ● ● ●

You might also choose to extend the loving kindness meditation to others that you care about.

● ● ● · ·

May you be well. May you be peaceful.
May you be loved. May you be truly happy.

· · ● ● ●

It's possible to extend this meditation further to include everyone that you know.

● ● · · ·

May we be filled with loving kindness.
May we be well. May we be peaceful.
May we be loved. May we be truly happy.

· · · ● ●

SUSTAINING YOUR MINDFULNESS PRACTICE

You know the evidence base for mindfulness. You're convinced by the benefits. Now what can you do to strengthen your commitment to practice? You might have the intention of practising daily for an hour but sometimes life gets in the way. It's normal to miss days or even weeks. This is when it's important to keep going. Begin again. Starting over is always an option with mindfulness.

- Listen to guided meditations. You can listen again and again. This is what guided meditations are for. You'll notice something different every time that you listen.

- Don't wait until everything is perfect. Sometimes you just need to make yourself sit and meditate. No time will ever be perfect.

- Use everyday moments for mindfulness. Whether it's walking, ironing, stretching or feeling the sun on your face – it's all an opportunity to be more mindful.

- Pay attention to your body throughout the day, bringing mindfulness to your physiology.

Remember that it takes time to build a habit. Be kind to yourself. If you do sixty seconds, it's an achievement. Congratulate yourself. If sixty seconds is sustainable for you, begin there. Keep it realistic.

Think of your life as the landscape for mindfulness. Bring mindfulness to your interactions with colleagues, friends and family. If you can't stick to the same time every day, you can incorporate mindfulness into *everything*. Let life be your meditation cushion. Think of mindfulness as a portable state of mind instead.

◆ FINDING A TEACHER ◆

When you're looking for a mindfulness teacher, it's important to check out the good practice guidelines recommended by the governing body in your country. Most countries will have a body that lists these.

Your teacher should have a regular mindfulness practice. It's okay to ask about this. You probably wouldn't choose a personal trainer who didn't exercise. Use the same principle for your mind. What training have they completed? Are there people who are able to recommend them?

Do they walk their talk? Known as embodiment, your teacher's actions should be consistent with their words. More than anything else, a teacher should be someone who you feel comfortable with.

▲▲▲

TROUBLESHOOTING YOUR EXCUSES NOT TO PRACTISE MINDFULNESS

I don't have time. Remind yourself of the Zen saying, 'You should sit in meditation for twenty minutes a day. Unless you're too busy, then you should sit for an hour.' Find ways to build mindful moments into your day. Take a look at 'Mindfulness for When You're Too Busy' (page 99–106). If adding mindfulness to your expanding 'to do' list feels overwhelming, it genuinely might not be the best time for you.

I can't do it. This is such an easy fix. There is no goal with mindfulness. You're not trying to achieve anything. Whatever happens, happens. If you get distracted, bring your focus back to the breath. There's an old Zen saying about hitting a piece of wood with an axe ninety-nine times. It splits on the one hundredth strike of the axe. It's like that with mindfulness. Keep trying. You'll get it.

I get distracted. That's kind of the point – you're training your brain so that it's easier to notice when distraction happens. Well done – you're already mindful. Let go of any expectations of what mindfulness 'should' be like. Don't expect to empty your mind. You will feel restless and you'll definitely have thoughts. That's part of meditation.

I'm way too stressed. Now, this excuse is an interesting choice. Mindfulness will reduce your stress levels but it's understandable that you might not want to examine that stress. If the thought of being mindful is adding to your stress – don't do it. There's always the option of working around the edges of stress. Bring your attention to what that stress feels like in the body, how it's showing up for you. Notice the thoughts that accompany it. Invite those thoughts in rather than pushing them away. Recognize that the stress is not 'you', that you are not your thoughts. If that doesn't work, take a mindful walk instead. Time in nature will offer up a fresh perspective. You can start anew tomorrow.

It takes too long to see benefits. Not true. Research shows that we can begin to see the benefits of mindfulness within six weeks.

I don't want to be passive. Mindfulness isn't about giving up or accepting the inevitable. It isn't about passive acceptance. Mindfulness allows us to respond effectively to emotions, rather than being their slave. When we practise mindfulness, it can help us to use emotions like anger to bring about social change, or to redirect our behaviour to resolve difficulties.

Mindfulness is way too pink and fluffy for me. Jokes about 'knitted yoghurt' aside, mindfulness has a robust evidence base. We know that it dampens down the activity in our amygdala and reduces cortisol in the body. Researchers have found that your immune system will be improved along with your ability to focus. Your memory will improve and you might just find that you feel happier and more content. The yoghurt, however, is optional.

▲▲▲

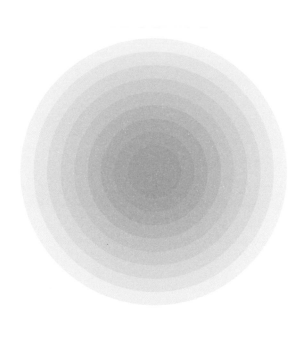

SUPPORTING RESOURCES

A WAY OF RECENTERING OURSELVES

Kabat-Zinn, J., *Full Catastrophe Living*. Piatkus, 2013.

Krauze, L., The Untold Story of America's Mindfulness Movement
tricycle.org/trikedaily/untold-story-america-mindfulness-movement/

Lu, S., Mindfulness holds promise for treating depression.
www.apa.org/monitor/2015/03/cover-mindfulness

McGreevey, S., Eight weeks to a better brain. How mindfulness increases grey matter in the brain.
news.harvard.edu/gazette/story/2011/01/eight-weeks-to-a-better-brain/

Pikörn, I., The Science of Mindfulness Part 2: The Historical and Conceptual Foundations of Mindfulness.
insighttimer.com/blog/the-historical-and-conceptual-foundations-of-mindfulness/

Purser, Ron, *McMindfulness: How mindfulness became the new capitalist spirituality*. Repeater Books, 2019.

Raichle, M. E. et al., A default mode of brain function
www.pnas.org/content/98/2/676.abstract

UK Good Practice Guidelines
bamba.org.uk/

YOUR BRAIN ON MINDFULNESS

Hanson, R, *Hardwiring Happiness: How to reshape your brain and your life.* Rider, 2014.

Ireland, T., What Does Mindfulness Meditation Do to Your Brain?
blogs.scientificamerican.com/guest-blog/what-does-mindfulness-meditation-do-to-your-brain/

Lazar, S., How Meditation Can Reshape Our Brains.
www.youtube.com/watch?v=m8rRzTtP7Tc

Worral, S., Why the brain-body connection is more important than we think.
www.nationalgeographic.com/news/2018/03/why-the-brain-body-connection-is-more-important-than-we-think/

The Center for Healthy Minds
centerhealthyminds.org/

GETTING DOWN TO MINDFULNESS

Norris, C. J., Creem, D., Hendler, R. and Kober, H., Brief
Mindfulness Meditation Improves Attention in Novices:
Evidence From ERPs and Moderation by Neuroticism.
www.frontiersin.org/articles/10.3389/fnhum.2018.00315/full

Puddicom, A., All it takes is 10 mindful minutes.
www.youtube.com/watch?v=qzR62JJCMBQ

LIVING IN THE PRESENT MOMENT

Hunt, M. G., Marx, R., Lipson, C. and Young, J., No More
FOMO: Limiting Social Media Decreases Loneliness and
Depression. Journal of Social and Clinical Psychology.
guilfordjournals.com/doi/10.1521/jscp.2018.37.10.751

Shayka, H. B. and Christakis, N. A., Association of Facebook
Use With Compromised Wellbeing: A Longitudinal Study.
American Journal of Epidemiology, 2017.
www.semanticscholar.org/paper/Association-of-Facebook-
Use-With-Compromised-A-Shakya-Christakis/5270606de
c382cfd50e925467ba35dac44654fc1

SUPPORTING RESOURCES

MINDFULNESS AND COMPASSION

Neff, K., Self-Compassion
self-compassion.org

Salzberg, S., Real Love: The Art of Mindful Connection.
Talks at Google.
www.youtube.com/watch?v=LML17BRZppU

Walker, M., *Why We Sleep: The New Science of Sleep and Dreams*. Penguin, 2018.

ACT With Compassion
www.actwithcompassion.com/homeworks

CALMING ANXIETY WITH MINDFULNESS

Smith, D. B., *Monkey Mind: A Memoir of Anxiety*. Simon & Schuster, 2013.

Mindfulness Meditation May Ease Anxiety.
www.health.harvard.edu/blog/mindfulness-meditation-may-ease-anxiety-mental-stress-201401086967

MINDFULNESS AT WORK

Edmondson, A. C., Learning from Mistakes is Easier Said Than Done: Group and Organizational Influences on the Detection and Correction of Human Error journals. sagepub.com/doi/abs/10.1177/0021886396321001

Kabat-Zinn, J., Mindfulness at Google. www.youtube.com/watch?v=3nwwKbM_vJc

Tan, C. M., *Search Inside Yourself: The Unexpected Path to Achieving Success, Happiness (and World Peace)*. HarperOne, 2014.

Google's Search Inside Yourself Adviser Mirabai Bush on Working with Mindfulness. www.youtube.com/watch?v=mHsMan_vauA

MINDFULNESS FOR WHEN YOU'RE TOO BUSY

Dweck, C., *Mindset: Changing the Way You Think to Fulfil Your Potential*. Robinson, 2017.

Escarao, M., Modern Mindfulness for Today's Busy World. www.youtube.com/watch?v=IzmDG0R3DRk

Thackray, G., *The Positivity Coach*. Michael O'Mara Books, 2020.

Thích N. H., *How to eat*. Rider, 2016.

CREATING A SUSTAINABLE, MINDFUL LIFE

Ricard, M., *Happiness: A Guide to Developing Life's Most Important Skill*. Atlantic Books, 2015.

Salzberg, S., *Real Change: Mindfulness to Heal Ourselves and the World*. Flatiron Books, 2020.

Wax, R., *Mindfulness Guide for the Frazzled*. Penguin, 2016.

William, M. and Penman, D., *Mindfulness: A practical guide to finding peace in a frantic world*. Piatkus, 2011.

▲ ▲ ▲

ABOUT THE AUTHOR

Gill Thackray has lived and worked around the world as a performance psychologist, coach, consultant and trainer. She now lives in the Lake District in the UK and when not there, spends as much time as possible in Paris. She has been a visitor and sometimes resident of the same street, Rue Ordener in Montmartre, for the last twenty years. In her spare time, she writes about the history of the street and the 18th arrondissement of Paris at 'Zen and the Art of Being in Paris'.

You can find Gill at:

www.korudevelopment.com
Twitter @KoruDevelopment
Instagram @korudevelopment
www.zenandtheartofbeinginparis.com

▲ ▲▲